Brendan's Journey

by
Gillette Elvgren Jr.

Published by
Blue Moon Press

For that Once-In-A-Blue-Moon Production

ISBN 978-1-943416-09-7

Printed in USA
Published by Blue Moon Plays

Brendan's Journey

CHARACTERS

BRENDAN..a fifth century monk.

BIRT..Brendon's companion.

Setting: Basically a bare stage. A projection screen/ ships sail can be artfully displayed, and most of the props, like a ladder, a sheepskin, and various hand props can be 'found'. It is also recommended that a sort of Bunraku stage hand be available to move stage pieces around, dressed in black. The two actors play various characters throughout the journey, aided by props and costumes.

ACT ONE

(Lights up. Large sail, half on floor of stage, half raised on a crossbeam with ropes and is clearly visible. The sail has a bulge in it. Fog. Old Irish music. Downstage a barrel with a candle and holder, a large book, other props as needed, a slide projector, tape recorder, and a glass of water. The sail will be used as a screen to project the slide images on. BIRT is standing there, a peasant, holding a scroll in his hand, looking as if he has just been awakened.)

BIRT: This be the story of...

(Sighs. Looks back at the bulge that is wrapped in the sail. Takes a drink out of the earthen cup. Opens scroll but doesn't read it.)

The story of Brendan, born in the year of our Lord 483, in the district north of Tralee east of Dingle in Eire, green Ireland, jewel of the sea, mother lode to high breasted red haired women, Tommy boy tenors, and every use of the potato that one can know-- where the sun shines but rarely on the thyme and the tansy, and where poor lads like me were breech-birthed in wattle huts across the river, always across, on the other side.

(The "bulge" stirs.)

In the year of our Lord, 483. St. Patrick himself, standing atop a hill in Limerick, his hand stretched across the sea, foretold it:

(BIRT puts on a long white yarn beard. Raises his hand. Sound effect of wind and surf.)

"Shine-you Shannon, for across your waves soon to be,
A wee laddie born will conquer thee,
And sail far out on the foam flecked sea,
God torn, Christ driven, Spirit blown he'll be."

(He off-handedly gestures to have sound cut off. He has obviously done this before. Takes off beard. Checks bulge, speaks confidentially.)

BIRT: Birt here.

(Gestures towards bulge.)

He calls me "Birt-dog when he's in a mood. "Dung heap", when he's not. You see, he was born a top the hill, I was born below. He had the fresh air, I had the bog and the smell of root and rot. He was held at the soft breast of his mother Cara, I split me Mum in two on my way out and was laid next to the black black dog by the hearth. Me father Fenn carried their buckets, you see, carried their slops, down the hill for a penny. Heap a dung. I knew BI Brendan first by his smell.

(*More demonstrative move from bulge.*)

Be that as it may...it was the year 483...

(*He unrolls BRENDAN downstage, out of the sail. BRENDAN is in monks robes, a little blinded by the light. Music accompanies this unveiling.*)

Brendan, son of Cara and Finnloag, one of the chosen of God, born atop a hill in Eire, swaddled in a windinq sail-- they say the forest about was afire with light. .

BRENDAN: Born in the middle of a miracle. Cara's breasts shone like snow.

BIRT: It's true, my father saw.

(A look from BRENDAN.)

BRENDAN: Saw what?

BIRT: Er. . .Saw the light, nothin' else-- saw the forest all lit up. My father wasn't one to stand gawking at a woman's window after dark. Brendan and me, we were born the same night. Him to the light, me to the darkness, and blood, and shadows and loss...

BRENDAN: The light. To see it manifest once again. For I ask you...

BIRT: Here we go.

BRENDAN: How can an incorporeal light burn corporeally in a corporeal creature?

BIRT: He tried to explain it once but it weren't no use. I'd rather chew on a root.

BRENDAN: Have you not heard of the bush burning at Sinai, yet the bush was unaffected by the fire?

BIRT: I've heard. Now if you talked of St. Elmo's fire off Mizen Head--zap! Topsail aglow in the rain driven snow, hair standing on end--zap! Conduit to the natural elements-Whoosh! Zap!

BRENDAN: You won't learn, will you Birt?

BIRT: I'm here aren't I?

BRENDAN: The question of God's holiness dwelling within...

BIRT: I survived, didn't I?

BRENDAN: The unquenchable fire...

BIRT: I survived you-- that's enough miracle for me.

BRENDAN: The light...

BIRT: You keep your light. I grow moss on the northside, the side away from the light-- see. I've never seen my toes. Clods to clods. I was sired to empty your chamber pot like my father and his before him. Let it be Brendan.

BRENDAN: Never.

(*Silence. A stand off. BRENDAN goes to slide projector remote control. First slide appears. BIRT raises sail a bit to catch slide image. Like all of the slides they are woodcut drawings that resemble the folk-art renderings so prevalent in illustrated books during the middle ages and after. The first slide is of a small dwelling, a woman.*

On the projection, CARA is standing in the doorway holding a babe in her arms. An old priest figure with a staff is standing before her. In the background watching is a deer with antlers. BRENDAN picks up a stick that he will use to lecture with.)

BRENDAN: Travels with Brendan. Back in the mists of early time, when Christ's light was but a glimmer, a beacon beckoning men...
(*Groan from BIRT*)
set in the Irish sea, a place where heathens hung idols at their hearth and wrapped themselves in fear, was born in the middle of a...

BIRT: We've done that. (*Pause*) We've done the birth bit B. I covered it.

(*Pause*)

BRENDAN: I had suckled at my mother's burning breasts for nigh on one year when, like the ancient story of Hannah and young Samuel, the Bishop Erc came to claim me for our Lord. It was said that Erc had been weaned from the Druids by holy Patrick himself.

(He has gestured with his stick to the figure in the slide. BRENDAN has picked up a small bundle. BIRT appears as the BISHOP ERC with robes made from animal skins and a headpiece of woven leaves and branches. BRENDAN as CARA, holds a 'bundle' and takes up a shawl.)

BRENDAN/CARA: Now remember, he doesn't like dirt. Dirt under his nails, dirt between his toes.

BIRT/ERC: Errrrr. He'll have to get his hands dirty with the Gospel. Helping the blind to see, the lame to walk-- it's not a clean business-- full of sweat and vinegar and spittle.

BRENDAN/CARA: He's not fully weaned. I suspect I'll have to come by. He'll suckle from no other, 'cept the doe.

(He runs and gestures to deer in slide.)

Hinds milk he'll take. Likes to look deep in their eyes.

BIRT/ERC: Arrrgh! He'll eat gruel and fat drippings and sprouts till his ears turn green.

BRENDAN/CARA: And he likes to be rocked, like this, and he seems inclined toward the sea. He shakes when he gets close enough to smell the salt air, and his little hands start to move...

BIRT/ERC: We don't swim in our order. We don't bath either. No, he'll stay dry. He'll gather twigs and sleep on dead leaves from the rowan tree.

BRENDAN/CARA: Oh, I don't...

BIRT/ERC: Ach, let him be. He'll drown in your dugs woman. Now some might say that's a sweet way to go, but with us he'll grow hard like stone and tall like the oak and crisscross the land like the ley lines of old winning souls to that great Druid high priest himself, the Kingly Cristos. Now give him here.

(ERC takes the child. BRENDAN clicks another slide. This one is a drawing of a monastery with a tree growing outside, a well on

the inside of the wall, a picture of old ERC with the boy BRENDAN, at his feet.)

BRENDAN: To the monastery, which was built in a grove of oaks...

BIRT/ERC: A sacred grove.

BRENDAN: Surrounded by a caer of monoliths, located atop an ancient tumuli...

BIRT/ERC: Fifteen hundred years of Celt, Gaels, Belgae, Druid, Briton, Roman...screaming from the earth, here, layer upon layer of holy bones, some broke, some burnt, some buried alive, and all crying for salvation, one voice...

(*BRENDAN becomes ten years old.*)

BRENDAN: And salvation be unto the Lord.

BIRT/ERC: (*pause)* Ahhhl Yes.

BRENDAN: Through his Son, Jesus the Christ.

BIRT/ERC: Mmmmmm. Stand still, boy. Eternal truths demand reverence. Reverence demands stillness. Stillness begets understanding, and understanding requires little more than a slight nod of the head-- thus.

BRENDAN: Yes.

(*He stands but begins to turn in a circle, counterclockwise. ERC cuffs him.)*

BIRT/ERC: Widdershins-widdershins! Turn the other way boy, if you must. Yer goin' 'gainst the sun. The moon'll pull counter -the- clock, yer blood'll run upstream, the heart'll lapse, you'll give a cold hand shake, clammy, premonition of death.

BRENDAN: I'll stand still if you'll tell me the story of the storm becalmed by the hand of God's son.

BIRT/ERC: Alright. Now sit.

(*BRENDON sits at his feet.*)

It was out of Sligo, off Donegal Bay that Jesus said to the twelve: "We sail lads, for Downpatrick's Head," and as the curragh set out for sea, our Lord rested his head on rope and creel and went fast asleep. It wasn't long, however, 'till Peter pointed aft and said, "Look mates, storm a gatherin'." Now what was the first thinq he did wrong?

BRENDAN: You don't point when you're at sea-- it's bad luck.

BIRT/ERC: Bad luck it was, and so, as soon as it were done he should of what?

BRENDAN: Held up his thumb and crossed his fingers thus.

BIRT/ERC: Ay, but in the panic of the moment he forgot. It was Tip-Tod's day.

BRENDAN: Friday, the devil's day.

BIRT/ERC: And the wind was out of the East, and we all know...

BRENDAN: "When the wind is in the East, it's good for neither man nor beast."

BIRT/ERC: Andrew was counting the waves.

BRENDAN: "Watch out for number seven."

BIRT/ERC: And James, he called for a caul.

BRENDAN: Caul?

BIRT/ERC. At birth, it's the membrane what covers some baby's head. You peel it off and you dry it out. It be the most precious of charms. I've known winter fisherman out of Omagh to pay a gold coin for one.

(*He whistles.*)

BRENDAN: You never whistle at sea.

BIRT/ERC: Aye. And as the waves crashed and the wind howled ditties from hell, and there was much quaking and gnashing of teeth, the men turned to the only help that was left.

BRENDAN: "Master, Master, we are sinking. Wake up!"

BIRT/ERC: And he did just that. Looked around. Scratched himself here. Rubbed his left eye thus, and spoke in the most gentlest of voices:

BRENDAN: Quiet down, storm.

BIRT/ERC: And it did just that.

BRENDAN: Yes.

(*Pause.*)

BOTH: " Oh ye of little faith."

BIRT/ERC: And they turned to each other, knowing now that the waves and wind and sky and stars and rocky crags themselves had ears and listened to His voice. "Who is this man?"

BRENDAN: I know.

BIRT/ERC: You're movin'.

BRENDAN: I don't want to grow roots. I want to sail out of Donegal Bay and ride the sea as Jesus strode the hills of Galilee. I want my order to sit astride the waves, not rot away in some kells or caves. Look, I wash between my toes twice a day to keep the dirt and dust away. I want to chase the sun, west, over the sea, for that will be my promised land.

(*ERC cuffs him, he falls, head pulled up to knees.*)

BIRT/ERC: (*Gently.*) "And when the wind is in the west then 'tis at its very best."

(*BRENDAN rises, brings up another slide. In it BRENDAN is seen praying while in the background Nuns are dancing, The tree of the garden is there with a serpent in the branches.*)

BRENDAN: If I was drawn to the sea I was also drawn to them.
(*Points to dancing nuns.*)
Torn from my mother's breasts, too young, Oh, they dressed from head to toe but the movement, underneath, caught the eye, then the mind. God made them with such curves, curves to be mindful of... Oh, the curse of all the in-between moments, bending over wash, scratching the neck, hand at

the hair like this, standing thus, stretching for apples, stretching, murmurs and laughter and hints and promises... And the way they danced.
It was the Abbess Ita who taught me to sail. (*Laughter from BIRT off.*) They call her the suckling Abbess-- taking in strays and orphans. Twenty-three years and she's never run dry. Other's say that she is the hind herself who watches in the forest glen for abandoned children. And still others say that she's a Gypsy and worships the Divine Mother of all existence until, like Paul on the road to Damascus, she met the living God on Wicklow Mount.

(*Music has been getting louder. ITA, played by BIRT, swirls on stage, huge black skirts that seem to take up the entire stage, she looks like a ship. Her white wimple atop her head stretched out three feet on each side, looking like a great white gull. She holds her arms out.)*

BIRT/ITA: Dordi Chavi...come to your Diddikai
(*She embraces him to her bosom. He almost suffocates.*)
Yes, I can feel, you are becoming such a little mus, soon you will be desiring a red-haired rackli, but that is no good for you, no kushti. Come, I will teach you to sail so that you can travel far away from all that is mochardi, from o Bengh who lurks around every corner, so the eye will see only the curve of wave, and the great Yog that God has caused to dwell within shall never be quenched.
(*Colorful ribbons are tied to her dress and the tips of the wings of her habit. They will act as ropes in the "sailing-dance" that is about to take place. Music up.)*
Here, take these. Wrap 'em tight and don't let go. Today we sail into the wind on a single-masted double-ended cog. Turn about, feel the wind blowing aft, let the boom find its place, tighter now, let her come round, round again, and hold it tight I said. Let her out, let her run, run before the wind and come about-- tack, down and up, up and down-- leeward and back again. Whew! You've made the run lad. If you was older we'd make our way to the Kitchemir for a pint o' Old Peculiar. Let me fan your face my red haired Dordi.

(*With her back to the audience she lifts her skirts to fan BRENDAN who is kneeling in front of her. He climbs out from under her skirts towards the audience.*)

BRENDAN: I was ashamed. I stuffed nettles down my shirt and rolled in seashells. "Oh Jesu, forgive me my sins of eye, ear and nose. Surround me in the morning mist of your mercy, let me wake from here on to the cry of the white gull, the flap of shiners on the flat windless tide, know the secrets of my heart as you know the heartbeat of the Leviathan in fathoms deep. For what I have seen strike me not blind, take not thy Holiest of Spirits from me, for I will serve you all the days and nights, dawns and dusks of my life."

(*He begins to move strangely in place. This will be a characteristic that will mark him for the rest of the play.*)

You see? He gave me my sea legs before I'd gone to sea. I pitched and rolled over hill and dale as if I were walking the deck of some cache out of Belmullet. The whole earth yawned and pitched, swerved and swayed. Brother Jarlath called it demon possession. Bishop Erc tried to get me to read the clouds on the horizon-- I needed a point of reference he said. The Abbess hung ropes from my shoulders to drag in the earth and slow me down, like they do a currach coming home in a gale. Bishop Erc christened me with gooseberry juice.

(*BIRT pours some juice over BRENDAN from a small paper cup.*)

But I escaped to the sea and took my real baptism there among the wee phosphorus creatures and the salty brine which tasted of tears and of blood. My sister Briga was nearby. She had taken to the sea also. She mended the fishermen's nets and she gave what she had to feed those of lesser means. It was with her alone her that I found peace.

(*Slide of a young maiden with nets about her, the sea and fisherman in the background. BRIGA/BIRT enters with a net. He wears a shawl.*)

BIRT/BRIGA: I thought I'd find you here. Could you hold this end?

BRENDAN: No. I can't sit still. I'm too full of Him.

BIRT/BRIGA: It's a blessing.

BRENDAN: A curse. How do you do it?

BIRT/BRIGA: What? Fix nets?

BRENDAN: Yes, that and everything else you do.

BIRT/BRIGA: I don't think about it.

BRENDAN: I think about everything.

BIRT/BRIGA: I wasn't born in the middle of a miracle.

BRENDAN: I want to know what it's like to wonder about little things, day to day things.

BIRT/BRIGA: Hold the net and I'll tell you. (*He takes net. Takes a large breath, almost collapses.*) Finnloag had me go down the hill and visit Fenn the other day. Birt was there, on the edge, he peeked at me around corners, you know how dark it is in the hollow. It was Samains, first fruits, mother had baked bread, some cheese. They have so little. Fenn took me aside and asked me to look deep in Birt's eyes and to tell me what I saw. So I did.

(*Pause.*)

BRENDAN: And...?

BIRT/BRIGA: I saw a man who climbed a hill and went down again. I saw a man who lived in wetness so that his skin was always wrinkled. I saw a man who'd go to sea, who'd know the wind and the sun. I saw a man who loved and... I saw us and I was frightened.

(*Jumps up.*)

BRENDAN: Why do you say that?

BIRT/BRIGA: That's what I saw.

BRENDAN: (*Breaking out of past character.*) You've never said that before. The healing, we're supposed to go on to the healing.

BIRT: But I was there.

BRENDAN: I know, but as yourself' not as her. Some things you can't know. .

BIRT: Some things I haven't said yet, not everything is told.

BRENDAN: The net, her quiet, I need that. There is a certain progression, a certain way of telling the story-- we agreed.

BIRT: Just like a fathom has a certain depth, or a knot has a certain speed?

BRENDAN: (*Loudly*) Yes!

(Pause. BIRT turns away, softens, and, with a shawl, once again becomes BRIGA.)

BIRT/BRIGA: I heard about the Miller's boy? Our Lord must be getting ready to send YOU out Brendan.

BRENDAN: I didn't do anything.

BIRT/BRIGA: That's not what they are saying up and down the coast.

BRENDAN: What are they saying?

BIRT/BRIGA: They are saying that you raised the Miller's boy from the dead. They wonder if you are Patrick come back from the grave.

BRENDAN: It's those kind of things...all I really want to do is go to sea.

BIRT/BRIGA: So what did happen?

BRENDAN: The funeral cortege had stopped, the wagon had a broken wheel and the casket had slipped head down and thrown the cover partially off. You could see the boy's head, all white, like dough. His clothes were white too. They were still covered with flour, the Miller hadn't even changed the boys clothes. I moved toward him, you know, to help right the box, cover him up, and since one arm was out, hanging outside, I touched him as I went to put it back inside. I was thinking of bread . . . or something. Then he sat up. He came back from the dead and I was thinking about supper.

BIRT/BRIGA: But you touched him?

BRENDAN: I wasn't the only one there.

BIRT/BRIGA: They say he embraced you and called you Lord.

BRENDAN: I was the closest. He got flour all over my cassock.

BIRT/BRIGA: They call you the Holy Monk.

BRENDAN: I'm not that. I'm not ordained. My first miracle was an accident. What does that portend for the rest of my life?

BIRT/BRIGA: Perhaps you shouldn't go to sea after all.

BRENDAN: What!

(*BRIGA laughs.*)

BIRT/BRIGA: You've forgotten how to laugh, Brendan.

BRENDAN: I never learned.

BIRT/BRIGA: Do you feel that the saint's of God are forbidden to laugh.

BRENDAN: No! You're younger than I, how can you ask me questions like that?

BIRT/BRIGA: I don't know.

BRENDAN: What's it like just to be?

BIRT/BRIGA: You're hungry, you eat. You're tired, you sleep. You're happy, you laugh.

BRENDAN: It isn't like that with me. You're hungry, you feel guilty about eating. Unless your words are songs of praise to God you feel your breath is wasted. You see a girl and you run in the other direction. I am driven. You just are. How I long for that.

BIRT/BRIGA: Learn to be happy for small things, Brendan. Come dance with me.

BRENDAN: I don't know how.

BIRT/BRIGA: I'll show you.

BRENDAN: No.

BIRT/BRIGA: Oh, Brendan, don't be so serious. I sleep in the sun, you want to chase it towards some Elysium beyond the rim of the western ocean. I want to have children, you want to convert them. Let God do what he will, you won't be able to hurry HIM up.

(*Shaking net, which she is fixing.*)

Hold it up.

BRENDAN: You think about having children?

BIRT/BRIGA: Sometimes.

BRENDAN: And do you think about having a husband?

BIRT/BRIGA: Of course I do.

BRENDAN: What do you think about?

BIRT/BRIGA: I think of a man, taller than you perhaps, who works in the woods, and whose arms are strong. He comes home with the setting of the sun and I can smell the earth on him-- the trees and the leaves, bark and berry. And I have cooked him dinner. In the evening we sit by the fire and tell stories to all the children, and watch as each falls asleep. We carry them to bed and then he carries me, and holds me in his strong, strong arms.

(*BRENDAN has covered his ears. BRIGA shakes her head and smiles.*)

BRENDAN: You're teasing. I don't like it.

BIRT/BRIGA: Then don't ask me if it bothers you so much.

BRENDAN: I'll ask whatever I like, and listen too.

BIRT/BRIGA: Yes, until you don't like it. Then you'll hide your head in your cowl like a turtle.

BRENDAN: So, is there someone special that I should know about?

BIRT/BRIGA: I'm thirteen, Brendan.

BRENDAN: Jenns was married at fourteen.

BIRT/BRIGA: She was ready.

BRENDAN: I want to know. We don't keep anything from each other.

BIRT/BRIGA: Alright! (*Pause.*) Kerry picked me up and twirled me around.

BRENDAN: Kerry?

BIRT/BRIGA: Linden. The third son of Bran Linden.

BRENDAN: He picked you up?

BIRTJBRIGA: He said, "I'll give you two years, lass." Then he set me down.

BRENDAN: And I suppose you noticed his strong arms.

BIRT/BRIGA: Yes, I did. But he doesn't work in the forest. (*Pause.*) Birt brought me a rabbit he'd killed.

BRENDAN: Birt?

BIRT/BRIGA: He told me that whatever he caught in this one trap he would give to me.

BRENDAN: Father said stay away from him.

BIRT/BRIGA: He seems nice enough.

BRENDAN: He never washes.

BIRT/BRIGA: I've never noticed.

BRENDAN: If father knew.

BIRT/BRIGA: He skinned the rabbit.

BRENDAN: Stop seeing him, I forbid it.

BIRT/BRIGA: You can't forbid it!

(*BRENDAN throws net down and crosses away.*)

BRENDAN: I do! I do forbid it! You must never see him again. He comes from the darkness. He offers you food set before idols. He is an abomination before the Lord.

BIRT/BRIGA: He is not!

(*BRENDAN has collapsed, again his hands are over his ears. BIRT/BRIGA comes up slowly behind him and caresses his head.*)

For you have left father and mother and sister and brother for His sake, and what you shall receive shall be a hundredfold, a blessing from beyond the sea.

BRENDAN: (*Raises his head slowly.*) I didn't tell you. Last night, when the voices had stilled and when I could once more sit quietly before Him I looked over the ocean and saw Tir-Na-N-Og on his white horse riding over the tops of the waves and he beckoned to me with his sword. I am to keep watch, for every seventh year the land of promise will appear over the ocean to the west, and I shall sail there and he will reveal to me the land to which he will give his saints for a time and half a time

(*He yawns.*)

So, I must be ready. And I will take you, take you away from boys in the forest, and from the night, to a land in the west where the sun shall never set . . .

(*He falls asleep in BRIGA'S arms as she sings.*)

BIRT/BRIGA
"Brother, brother, never fear,
For God our helmsman watches o'er,
His son beside us, ever near,
As *we* travel to distant shore."

(*BIRT roughly drops him and the shawl. Stands.*)

BRENDAN: (*Still a bit dazed.*) So we began construction on a boat .

BIRT: Wrong. You're only twenty-three. First trip to Britain, Council at Whitby, all those Monks and Bishops huddled together discussing schisms and creeds. And to the East and South were the Saxon's, great hairy beasty men what devoured beachheads and maidenheads and who were looking to take over the entire country with their pagan ways.

BRENDAN: Aye. Three blessed barrels of saltwater. (*Points to a barrel.*) Birt, would you get those loaded.

BIRT: Wrong again. I hadn't started working for you yet. I was still back in Tralee digging tubers and chasing wild pigs in the forest. Load 'em yourself.

(*He exits.*)

BRENDAN: We sailed south at night, around Lands End and into the

Bristol Channel. We carried with us three barrels of saltwater, blessed by the Holy See, drawn from Abb's Head estuary, holy water to be used for its healing properties by Arthur, later to be misconstrued as King Arthur of Camelot fame, who was about to engage the heathens not far from the Salisbury Plains.

(Slide of clashing forces.)

BRENDAN: We crossed through Glastonbury. It was December and the staff of Joseph of Arimathaea at Wearyall was in bloom. On into Wiltshire and thus to Baden, Mount Baden if you could call it that-- a hill of sorts with a crude mud and wood fort atop. The Britons were under siege.

(BIRT playing ARTHUR comes on carrying a large cress on his back. Battle sounds.)

BIRT/ARTHUR: Don't bring out the horses yet! Keep 'em back till I give the word! Cerdic's no fool-- he'll be moving up the ravine right now-- pull the dams on the Cam and flood him out--do it!

(Sees BRENDAN.)

Who are you? What have you got?

BRENDAN: Holy water from the See at Whitby.

BIRT/ARTHUR: Here, hold this will you.

(Hands cross to BRENDAN. drinks greedily from the barrel.)

It's salt! What good is salt water? Where are you from?

BRENDAN: From Eire.

BIRT/ARTHUR: That's all I need-- apostate monks from across the channel. *(Yelling off.)* Fire! Put it out! Get it out, man. We've got three barrels of salt water here, use these.

BRENDAN: But this water is to be used to heal the wounds of the afflicted.

BIRT/ARTHUR: And if there is any left, wash down the horses.

BRENDAN: Holy water on horses?!

BIRT/ARTHUR: My horses are more important than any man right now. The Saxons and the Jutes think they're beasts from the underworld. It's the black of their coats and the red of their eye. We'll ride out on them at dusk. You watch. Careful, don't let that touch the ground, keep it upright man.

BRENDAN: It's heavy...

BIRT/ARTHUR: Stop whining. I got the horses in Arabia and since I wasn't too far away I stopped off in Jerusalem and I had it made-it's the same size as the one our Lord hauled to Golgotha. And here, you see this breastplate-- a picture of St. Mary Ever-Virgin at the foot of the cross, blessed by St. Bede himself. Do you believe me?

BRENDAN: I don't...

BIRT/ARTHUR: Never mind, it doesn't matter what you think, just as long as they believe. The cross? I picked that idea up from St. Moses and his holding up Aaron's rod and keeping back the waves over the red sea. It seems to be working. Here, take this... and this.

(*Puts helmet and breast plate on BRENDAN.*)

You want to play Saint? Here's your chance. You put it down, their blood be upon your head! I'll be asleep, and I don't want to be bothered. Just stand still-- in silhouette they'll think it's me-- Lord Arthur, Holy Artorius, Arthur soon-to-be King. Stand straight man. Every once in awhile yell: "forward" or "God, country and Arthur!" or just yell.

(*He starts to exit.*)

BRENDAN: Before you go -- one question. How can an incorporeal light burn corporeally on a corporeal creature?

BIRT/ARTHUR: What?

BRENDAN: Inside. How can God's light-Spirit burn within our human breasts?

BIRT/ARTHUR: God 's-Watch' are they all like you in fairy Eire? The only fire that burns in me is a hunger-- for food. I haven't eaten in two days. All I want is to grow old with my children on a farm in Somerset. I am here because the three Kings of Britain are paying me in gold and the promise of more horses. If we win today it will be a great victory for God. If we lose I let my hair grow and learn Saxon and rape and pillage with the best of them. Your concern now is to hold up that cross. Should it fall or waver I shall personally disembowel you from gullet to gut and then we shall have a first hand glimpse of this fire of yours.

(*ARTHUR runs off.*)

BRENDAN: The Lord was victorious at the Battle of Baden. Cerdic's forces were defeated. They retreated to the plains of East Anglia and became farmers. It was forty or fifty years before they began pushing West but by this time the Church had done its duty and Christianized the pagan hoard of Anglo's, Saxon's, Jutes and others. Arthur grew fat and was killed by his brother Mordred ten years later-- never to return again.

(*Pause. BRENDAN still holds cross. Looks around.*)

Birt!

(*Pause.*)

Birt dog!

(*BIRT enters as if he was asleep, scratching, yawning.*)

BIRT: What? Is it time for intermission?

BRENDAN: Get this off me.

(*Helping him get disentangled from ropes.*)

BIRT: I thought it would do you good-- the yoke of Christ an' all.

(*BIRT hauls cross off under one arm. BRENDAN pushes slide projector remote. Picture of Monks working, enclosed by a wood fence, a cross on a mud hut.*)

BRENDAN: Thirty years of age. Ordained. I founded my first monks cell in Magh Enna in Mayo. I named it Ardfert.

(*Gregorian Chant music. BIRT enters with straw broom.*)

BIRT: Hired me to work for three meals a day. These monks were good at being Holier -than-thou but not much good at cleaning up or washing down. They lived in caves and huts not far from the sea-- ate seaweed and potatoes that they grew in the cracks of the rocks where dirt had collected.

BRENDAN: We started with six. Within a year we were twelve.

BIRT: They lived off the guilt of those around. Squire Grumphie got Scotty Dodd's daughter pregnant. Gave him two pigs, gave the monastery an acre of land-- man and God were taken care of.

BRENDAN: The Bishop would not give me permission to sail so I took to the land.

BIRT: He made a vow not to face the ocean. Funny thing to see him walking along, crab-like, facing inland like this, but straining to catch the smell of the salt air.

BRENDAN: A monastic life requires strict discipline.

BIRT: (Contemptuously.) Rules and Regulations... If you're unsure or scared of something you keep the fear afar with a bunch of...

(*Waving a document which BRENDAN grabs and reads.*)

BRENDAN: Rule #1: We will observe silence until 1 p.m. Two-thirds of piety consists in the observance of silence.

BIRT: Creepy, all those grown men clammed up tighter than a barrel of codfish oil. Pretty soon everybody got good at talking with their hands. . .

(*He pantomimes the following with gestures, then says it.*)

Those . . . are my . . . carrots . . .. If you . . . eat another . . . I'll bust you up side of the face . . .

BRENDAN: We will sleep on floors.

BIRT: One brother named Janus digs a ditch three inches deep at floor level. Fills it with goose feathers and then covers it with his blanket. Slept the sleep of the dead, and looked like it too.

BRENDAN: Hospitality will be stressed.

BIRT: Oh right: gates closed until one due to vespers an' all; bunch of smelly monks trying to grow potatoes with wet rot and drink from sour grapes; sleep on the dirt-- I mean, the folks about Tralee are poor enough but nobody in their right mind is goin' to seek out hospitality there.

(*BRENDAN gives him a hard look.*)

And if you think he never smiled before.

(*He exits.*)

BRENDAN: And the Lord blessed us. Cell's founded soon after in Barrow, Tathoo, Kilfenora and Brandon Hill gathered to my Rule and I traveled from one to another, laying on hands, seeing that oratories were kept up and that the monks sang the Psalms in tune. The harvest was rich. Healing abounded. Many were instructed in how to read the Gospel. And in and through all I kept my back to the sea.

(*BIRT enters as BRIGA with shawl.*)

BIRT/BRIGA: And a shadow lay over half his face.

BRENDAN: Briga.

BIRT/BRIGA: It's been over a year, Brendan. The children have forgotten their Uncle. A man dressed in brown is all Shaun can remember.

BRENDAN: I couldn't come. I didn't know what to say.

BIRT/BRIGA: Kerry went out to sea and he never came back. It happens. It's over. I miss his strong arms but the little ones give me comfort.

BRENDAN: Why don't you join with Abbess Ita? You could still raise the children...

BIRT/BRIGA: No. I am too much of the world. I like sleeping late. I enjoy the stories and the laughter from the sailors in the evening.

BRENDAN: And our Lord...?

BIRT/BRIGA: God doesn't only reside in cells and monasteries, Brendan.

BRENDAN: I know that, I know. But the work that is being done here, Briga--every day we send out Missionaries-- to Iona, Clonfoish and Clonard, to the Western Isles and even back to Scots-land. We have harvesters galore, what is lacking are new fields where souls might be garnered for Christ.

BIRT/BRIGA: And what of you?

BRENDAN: Me?

BIRT/BRIGA: The incorporeal light?

BRENDAN: I run before God's Spirit with His song on my lips. Wherever I stand still for more than a minute, no a second, a church is founded and Saints of God are re-born from brittle earth and hard stone. Jehovah's face has turned upon the Irish countryside and the hills are alight with the presence of God!

BIRT/BRIGA: And what of Brendan whose back is turned towards the sea?

(*Pause. He deflates.*)

BRENDAN: Ashes.

(*BRIGA embraces him. Gently turns him around. A light makes his face glow.*)

BIRT/BRIGA: Then turn around. Follow the sun. A new harvest of souls is in the West, out there-- your own Promised Land.

(*He begins to smile, to respond to the light and warmth. Then he doubts.*)

BRENDAN: I'm...not sure. My work here...

BIRT/BRIGA: Can be done by others. I was sent here to tell you this.

BRENDAN: I will pray .

BIRT/BRIGA: Yourself into oblivion.

BRENDAN: I would need a curragh, no two or three. Supplies...

BIRT/BRIGA: It could take forever at this rate. (*Pause.*) Birt is building a cottage in the forest.

BRENDAN: Birt?

BIRT/BRIGA: He says that it's for me and the children.

BRENDAN: How could he? He works for me.

BIRT/BRIGA: Not on Mondays. On Mondays he builds his cottage. He's very strong.

BRENDAN: How often are you seeing him?

BIRT/BRIGA: On occasion.

BRENDAN: Too often. I'll insist he work seven days a week.

BIRT/BRIGA: He says this house is his passion.

BRENDAN: THAT'S not his passion.

(BRIGA shrugs.)

BIRT/BRIGA: I share a place now with two other families, women like myself... the children are getting bigger, we could use...

BRENDAN: He ' s not a believer.

BIRT/BRIGA: He has a good heart.

BRENDAN: There's many a good heart roasting in hell.

BIRT/BRIGA: He has two rooms finished. .

BRENDAN: You're right. I'll do it. We'l l start now, tomorrow. I'll chase the sun as I have chased lost souls here. The curraghs shall become our cells, floating cells, a brotherhood of the waves and wind. And Birt will come.

BIRT/BRIGA: I'm not sure. . . his father is ill.

BRENDAN: He'll come. He was born to be a joiner. He'll craft the boats. He'll have to come. We'll start gathering wood now . . poplar.

BIRT/BRIGA: Ash.

BRENDAN: And we'll sail by May. The lost shall be found. The dead will be given new life. (*Pause.)* Would you like something to eat?

(*She smiles. Shakes her head. Embraces him. Exits. Sound of hammer and sawing, of a boat being built. Slide of monks working on hull of boat. Animals watching. Distant figure of BIRT hauling wood. A stylized boat will be manufactured during the scene with an indication of a prow and the skeleton like ribbing of a hull. Also a rudder.*

To BIRT, noting the facsimile of tools which BIRT has carried on.)

One pincers, 2 awls, shovels, crimpers and flax. Is that it?

(*BIRT drops all.*)

BIRT: Aye. All in a litter.

BRENDAN: Ash lathes?

BIRT: I've got your ash.

BRENDAN: You're to stay here. Sleep there, on that mound of seaweed. Watch over the tools, the hides, one eye open...

BIRT: I've got my cottage...

BRENDAN: You're to stay down here. Watch the tide. The brothers will help.

BIRT: I get one day to work on my cottage.

BRENDAN: You'll build me one belly, one back of a boat that would put Noah to shame.

BIRT: Aye, I said I'd do it, but...

BRENDAN: Forget the hovel. Put it behind you. I've heard with my ears the song of our lovely sailorman, the nautical Christos.

BIRT: Well, I haven't heard a thing.

BRENDAN: And he's given me a vision of the Land of the Blessed, out there, where the rotten underside of sin has never been tasted, where death is only a faint echo on the wind, and where all you've ever desired and sought after and lost is discovered once again.

BIRT: I've got everything right here thank you.

BRENDAN: I see the sun...

BIRT: See what you like. All I see is a lot of back wrenching nail splittin' work for three meals a day and a bottle of ale.

(*Pause.*)

BRENDAN: I need you Birt.

BIRT: That's better.

BRENDAN: The brothers have grown cabbage, built a fence of sorts. Never anything like this. I need you to build me my boat.

BIRT: I'm listening.

BRENDAN: We'll sail west. It'll be a trial of sorts. A few days out, then back, 'till we get the hang of it. You decide whether you want to leave or come with us. Three meals and three coppers a day, but I'll need you for seven days a week, that'll give us four months to build this thing before we launch her in early May.

BIRT: Four coppers and Friar Joseph spends time with my sick father in the hollow.

BRENDAN: Agreed.

(The following sequence of work is done.)

BIRT: We fashioned the frame of white ash, it looked like the bleached bones of the Leviathan himself.

BRENDAN
(Singing)
"OH SAILORMAN, OH MY SAILORMAN
REACHING OUT ACROSS THE SEA,
TO THE HOLY LAND, THE HOLY LAND,
WE'LL SET OUT TO BE WITH THEE.

BIRT: He took up singing. When they all got going they sounded like a chorus of fallen angels. You see this? Heartwood of oak. Laid it down the gunwales. It'll bring boatyard luck.

BRENDAN:
MY CARPENTER, OH MY CARPENTER,
BLESS THIS AWL AND THIS NAIL,
TO THY PROMISED LAND, THY LOVELY LAND,
WE SHALL SOON SET THY SAIL.

BIRT: The main mast and the mizzen, also made from oak. I was taking no chances. When we laid the masts I guided them below, down into the hull to be lashed to the frame and crossbeams. He didn't see but I put a silver coin under each mast-- Briga gave them to me. More good luck.

BRENDAN:
MY CRUCIFIED, OH MY CRUCIFIED,
YOU HAVE SHED YOUR BLOOD FOR ME.
SO PROTECT ME LORD, OH PROTECT ME LORD,
FROM THE ANGER OF THE SEA.

BIRT: The hull was made from ox hides-- forty-nine of them, a quarter inch thick, four deep at the bow, two deep at the stern. We stripped them of hair in the lime pits and then scrapped them with knives. We tanned them in the syrup from the towering oak. That was my idea too. You could hear the cries and screams that came from it when it was felled. That means it was fully alive, which is what you want. You see the oak has many magical properties, not the least of them being protection from lightening, which is a good thing to have at sea. Then these hides were sewn to the skeleton of ash lathes with thongs soaked in salt water. You blister pushing it through, get stabbed on the other side-- my blood can be found from stem to stern. Theirs too, but more o' mine.

BRENDAN:
MY RISEN LORD, OH MY RISEN LORD,
LET OUR BOAT BE THY GRAIL,
HOLY SPIRIT COME, PRECIOUS SPIRIT COME,
AND PLEASE BLOW ON OUR SAIL.

BIRT: Now, you may ask yourselves, why a leather boat? It was not uncommon for the day-- the salt water had a pickling effect on the skins. And they were covered with liberal doses of wool grease. We were up to our elbows in wools fat. On a windy day they could smell us in Derry. It might of been as he said. .

BRENDAN: A pleasing scent unto our Lord.

BIRT: But they wouldn't let me into town to purchase supplies-made me stand at the edge of the green, downwind, with the bairns throwing rocks and sticks . . . It would be a foul stinkin' journey and I don't want any part of it.

BRENDAN: You've taken the coppers. You've eaten the food.

BIRT: To the Orkney's and back. Test her out.

BRENDAN: We'll need salt fish, three barrels, onions, flat loaves, dried fish and hazel nuts.

BIRT: I shoulda known when I saw him loading all the supplies.

BRENDAN: Another set of flax sheets, spare halyards, needles and thread. We sail tomorrow. "Let the Lord in heaven above rejoice in his works."

BIRT: His work! It was me who was bent double and who stunk to high heaven.

BRENDAN: (*Making the sign of the cross.*) In the name of the Father the Son, and the Holy Ghost I name *thee* Cara.

BIRT: After his old Mum. That night I broke a bottle of Barley malt across her bow and called her Briga after my love. It was the year of our Lord, 514 when we set sail. May sixteen...

BRENDAN: 514. Cast off. We sail for the legendary land of the Blessed. Our coracle is a great womb that will deliver us up upon the shores of the second Galilee.

BIRT: And if you be there, hidden someplace upon the bosky moors, or in the dank morning mist, deliver me from this mad monk and return me to the arms of my Briga dear.

BRENDAN: I'll search the watery desert for the *pax de Cristos,* for the savaged lost souls of time and space, I'll out Patrick Patrick himself among the froth and the fire of barren shores-- Let HIM be known. Oh, let HIM be known this day to all and forever more.

BIRT: Do you hear that! Five minutes at sea and he's already raving.

BRENDAN: Up foresail! Sheet to the starboard! Up! Up! and let her ride!

BIRT: Turn her about, I've changed my mind.

BRENDAN: It's too late. We're set now for the rim of the world-- no turning back.

BIRT: I'll swim to shore, Brendan.

BRENDAN: 5 coppers a day.

BIRT: Seven!

BRENDAN: What?

BIRT: Seven coppers.

BRENDAN: You'd take all that I have.

BIRT: Seven...

BRENDAN: All right! When we get back, you build your cottage in the glen. I won't stand in your way. You do what you must but the choice be hers. Remember this Birt Fenn, you live in the lichen, moss grows in your pit. She is a creature of the sun.

BIRT: She'll have me.

BRENDAN: We'll see. Then you'll pledge this voyage?

BIRT: I will. By all that's holy and sacred-- to me.

BRENDAN: (*BIRT raises sail.*) Don't swear. I won't have your heathen curses about. Put your boots on. Northeast. Hard by. Into the sun. Follow the sun

(They sing in harmony.)

OH SAILORMAN, OH MY SAILORMAN,
REACHING OUT ACROSS THE SEA.
TO THE HOLY LAND, THE HOLY LAND,
WE'LL SET OUT TO BE WITH THEE.

(Lights out. End of Act I.)

ACT II

(*Lights up. Special on BIRT. Upstage BRENDAN is seen standing on a barrel silhouetted against the sail, arms outstretched, holding onto the cross mast or held by ropes. Slide of ship, roiling waves, several monks, head shaved, are seen on slide. Music segues into wave and wind sound.*)

BIRT: Fifteen days we sailed wither. Wither and non. None knows where 'cept the "Spirit," he says. Only it weren't us alone. Three brothers from his monastery tagged along. Some say twelve after the number of his Lord's disciples. They were trying to make a saint of him even back then. There was only three-- I was there. I couldn't tell them apart, Brother this, Brother that-- all brown, monk robed, shaven atop their pates, scurrying around like blind moles finding no earth to dig in. Eight days out they turned green. It was the flux. They hung their great asses over the side and propelled us along with the gasses they vented and with their piteous lamentations. Not him though. Lean as salted beef and just as hard. Runs the ship the same way he ran his cells-- half a day of silence, vespers, vigils, versicles-- him chanting "Praise the Lord, all his angels; praise him all his power," the three churls dragging their cheeks in the passing brine, and me bringing us about, hugging the rudder a nights, conjuring up visions of Briga tight in my arms.

(*BRENDAN stirs.*)

On the twenty-seventh day, the wind stopped.

(*BIRT gets out an oar and begins to row. BRENDAN comes down.*)

BRENDAN: What are you doing?

BIRT: What does it look like?

BRENDAN: Why?

BIRT: We're not moving, are we?

BRENDAN: So?

BIRT: (*Spits over the side.*) There it sits. No eddies, no tides to move it on. Well, a glob of spit may be content to idle itself away like that, but I'm not. What are you looking at? You would do better to roust those "brothers" of yours and put them to work on the other oars so we don't run in circles.

BRENDAN: And where are you taking us?

BIRT: "Into the sun." It's all you've talked about. On to the chosen lands, the promised paradise-- well it all sounds very nice but it takes a bit of sweat and a raw backside to make things happen, so be it. And, if I have to do it by myself so that I can the sooner return to the green of Eire, so be it. And if you have any idea of stopping me than strip to your waist Brendan Finnloag and we'll have at it like we did as boys in the hog wallow in Lock Lein. I had you then and I'll have you now. So just say the word and, SO BE IT!

(*BIRT is ready to fight. BRENDAN is disconcertingly calm.*)

BRENDAN: Brother, do not fear. God is our helper, sailor and helmsman, and he guides us. Ship all the oars and the rudder. Just leave the sail spread and God will do as he wishes with his servants and their ship.

(*BRENDAN takes the oar and is about to cast it overboard. BIRT grabs it.*)

BIRT: Oh no you don't.

BRENDAN: Give it up, Birt.

BIRT: Not on your life.

BRENDAN: Like Noah's Ark we'll be taken where we will.

BIRT: It's Birt's back that will take you where you will.
(He wrenches the oar from Brendan's grasp.)
And it's Birt's knowledge of the stars that will take you west until the last piece of salted cod has been swallowed by those gutless wonders back there and the turnips have turned to mush and you say, "turn back, the voyage is done, the dream has turned to ashes."

(*BRENDAN embraces him.*)

BRENDAN: I said, give it up!

(*BIRT fights himself loose, BRENDAN crosses towards the sail, fingering his cross and chanting softly in Latin.*)

BIRT: Oh, I know we're coming back. We sailed on the eve of the summer solstice-- he doesn't know. Tiptods day the Druid priest told me, the stars were in their right position. He's got his word and I've got mine.

BRENDAN: Land Ho!

(*Slide of island and dog greeting BRENDAN.*)

BIRT: We circle the island three times before we land on the third day at three in the afternoon. Brendan does everything in three's and seven 's. Three's were "propitious". Stepping on shore this dog comes along and leads us to a great hall. He was pissing as he went. The dog, not Brendan. I liked that.

BRENDAN: Make sure that none of you takes anything belonging to this island with him.

BIRT: Don't look at me!
(*To audience.*)
He was looking at me!
(*Back to BRENDAN.*)
I'm hauling water and trading salt cod for salt pork.
(*He is changing into a Monk's robe.)*
But one of the brothers, Cuthbert by name, was to filch a silver chalice from the banquet which the townspeople and the Lord of the Great Hall was to lay before us.

(*A chalice drops down from under the robes of BIRT who is playing CUTHBERT.*)

BRENDAN: Look, our Brethren who I warned so few days ago has given birth to a chalice.

BIRT/CUTHBERT: The devil, he enticed me.

BRENDAN: It was your hand that took it.

BIRT/CUTHBERT: It was as if I were a thing possessed.

BRENDAN: I know. But it was your thought that made it so.

BIRT/CUTHBERT: He tempted me.

BRENDAN: You desired.

BIRT/CUTHBERT: So which came first?

(*Speaks as BIRT.*)

They were always getting into arguments like this. Brendan cut this one short.

(*BRENDAN points to CUTHBERT, an incriminating gesture.*)

BRENDAN: You desired.

BIRT/CUTHBERT: Only once, in between the rack of lamb and the blood pudding. It wasn't really a thought, it was an ... afterthought.

BRENDAN: You ate too much.

BIRT/CUTHBERT: The cushions were too soft.

BRENDAN: Three glasses of Rhenish.

(*CUTHBERT fondles the chalice. Slightly drunk.*)

BIRT/CUTHBERT: Look, carved unicorns, and there. . . there's Bran stirring his great cauldron. I touched it here. .

(*He touches chalice with his tongue.*)

BRENDAN: A desultory gesture.

BIRT/CUTHBERT: A harmless fancy.

BRENDAN: At that moment you allowed him in.

BIRT/CUTHBERT: I said, "as if", "as if I was possessed," I never said.

BRENDAN: I saw him in a dream, an Ethiope entered in...

(*BIRT drops out of character.*)

BIRT: Wait just a minute. What do you mean by Ethiope?

BRENDAN: He was black. A black demon entered in.

BIRT: He? It was a man then?

BRENDAN: No.

BIRT: He wasn't a man?

BRENDAN: No, he was more like a creature. an "it"

BIRT: But like an Ethiope?

BRENDAN: It WAS black.

BIRT: But it wasn't actually an Ethiope?

BRENDAN: No, it was scales and fur. Red of eye-- it hissed.

BIRT: Would you say "black as night" then, or "black and bleak as a lost soul" or "black as the bile from the plague victims vomit," or "black as the pit of hell"?

BRENDAN: Yes, all of that.

BIRT: And might any of those be more appropriate than "Ethiope?"

(*BIRT gestures and BRENDAN looks at audience.*)

BRENDAN: I see what you mean.
(*Back in the scene with CUTHBERT, BRENDAN exhorts.)*
By the blood of our Lord, shed for the sins of all mankind -- come out!

(*BIRT has turned, put on a mask resembling one of the demon dancers in the Chinese Opera. He whirls about.*)

DEMON/BIRT: Why, man of God, do you expel me from my dwelling where I have lived and make me depart from my inheritance?

BRENDAN: I know we're not supposed to engage the likes of you in conversation, but I have question for you?

BIRT/DEMON: And what makes you think I'll answer?

BRENDAN: How is it that you, an incorporeal creature, could in-dwell the flesh?

BIRT/DEMON: Oh, I'll tell you that. You look for a cold spot, a deadness poised between the anvil of the will and the hammer of ones spirit, non-quickened, harkening back to the origin of sin itself. You nestle there and burn cold-- waiting.

BRENDAN: But how...where?

BIRT/DEMON: Oh, on the dark side of the spleen, where else? There, among the weakened links of lust and appetite and fear.

(*He begins to circle BRENDAN.*)

For even you, holy one, have unholy desires, dark longings. I see your sister, Briga of the long limbs, her face a white moon in folds of blackness, then his face...but whose?

BRENDAN: Stop!

BIRT/DEMON: You have room for more than one, holy man. There, I see it, a thin crack... just let go.

BRENDAN: No! I stand against... in the name of our Savior, I cast you out...away...be gone and I order you to injure no man to the day of judgement.

(The DEMON screams, turns away. BRENDAN sits, exhausted. In the back around BIRT is seen coiling a rope.)

BIRT: It's been three days since we've eaten meat, Brendan.

BRENDAN: We sail into the wind, ever West. We defy the order of nature. We chew on parsnips and hazelnuts, red of eye, joints swollen, as He takes us in that direction. During matins the ship is driven by "Holy, holy, holy Lord, God of power and might," rather than by the mind or arm, back, rudder, or current.

BIRT: Our teeth are falling out from chewing on this mush.

BRENDAN: At noones our chants of "Praise the Lord all his Angels, praise him all his powers," drives us on as surely as the wind. He truly makes for us a path in the wilderness of cap and wallow of wave.

(*All of a sudden BIRT is jerked and almost pulled offstage as the rope let's itself out. BRENDAN changes slide-- fight with a whale.*)

BIRT: I've got him. Grab on, Brendan.

(*BRENDAN does so.*)

BRENDAN: What is it?

BIRT: Leviathan on a leash spouting foam and flume-- whoosh! Whoosh again!

(*They are tossed about.*)

He's diving, going down. Down darkling, down.

BRENDAN: We're taking water on the leeboard side. He's ten times longer than the boat. We'll never...

BIRT: He's got to come up. He'll be ours.

BRENDAN: He'll drag us down to hell.

BIRT: He'll douse the fires.

BRENDAN: He's shifting. God man, what have you hooked?

BIRT: Breakfast, supper. . . skin, oil, bone. We'll winter in his belly.

BRENDAN: He's turning!

BIRT: I'll be your first convert Brendan, brought to our Lord on the mountainside of Leviathan's flesh, converted by a mouthful of liver, heart, gizzard, fin-- flesh!

BRENDAN: East! He's pulling us back.

BIRT: Easy, he'll turn again.

(*BRENDAN lets go.*)

Don't let go, man. Hang on. We've got him.

BRENDAN: West not East...

BIRT: Look, he's shifting back.

BRENDAN: I don't see...

BIRT: He will-- I can't hold him!

BRENDAN: It wasn't meant to be.

(The rope pulls out fast. BIRT screams as his hands are burned. Finally, he lets go and falls to the deck. BRENDAN kneels next to him, tenderly rubbing in salve. BIRT pulls away.)

BIRT: Don't touch me. You never were one to get your hands soiled. Hands soft as communion wafers.

BRENDAN: The Leviathan...

BIRT: Was on the end of my line.

BRENDAN: ...remains a mystery. It was a dream.

BIRT: Would have fed us.

BRENDAN: Consumed us.

BIRT: (*He spits.*) I'm hungry Brendan. That's all that burns within me. I can't live on matins and incense.

(*He takes a knife, cuts himself, howls, Puts a rag over the wound.*)

BRENDAN: My God, Birt.

BIRT: (*Suffering.*) Stay back. A bit of flesh to entice another bit of flesh, that's what it boils down to. A mackerel, say, tastes Birt's flesh. Birt brings him in, tastes him, her, saves a snatch of tail or head, casts out for some more. Dog eat dog. And so it goes on and on... we're all just eating each other, this way or that. .

(*He has been baiting a primitive rod, casts it over. BRENDAN moves downstage near projector, speaks to audience.)*

BRENDAN: Cuthbert died. He never survived the loss of the appetite, which was consuming him. To the end he remained a hollow vessel. Birt's immolation turned putrid. He'd trail his hand in the wake. There was fever. He had a dream.

(*Music continues. BRENDAN changes slide to that of a man flying with majestic wings.*)

BIRT: *(Slide of man flying with feathered wings. He moves as a great majestic bird.*) I lead a simple life I do. Thrust out of the nest at an early age, weaned from my Mum's nestle off the cliffs of Adele, took to the air, it's drafts and gullies, like it were part of me. Never landed. Seven years now, feet tucked up so, imagine they've atrophied some time back from lack of use. I skim the bays of Laird snapping up shiners flashing their bellies, make love on the wing, at night with the phosphorescence twinkling below, stars overhead, like a dream.

(*BRENDAN, wearing a shawl, appears as BRIGA.*)

BRENDAN /BR I GA: Come down, Birt. It's Briga.

(*BIRT jumps from a barrel. Walks unsteadily.*)

BIRT: There. Better be good Briga. Seven years on the lamb. Look at me! I'm a sitting duck 'till I find a cliff face and can be launched again. I didn't mean for you to view me so... out of sorts...

(*He hides his bandaged hand.*)

I belong up there in the eddies and the currents.

BRENDAN/BRIGA: Your arms, so large...

BIRT: Like I said, seven years on the wing-- don't imagine they're much good for more than this. . (*He flaps them.*) ...after all that time.

BRENDAN/BRIGA: And the cottage in the forest...?

BIRT: Half covered with moss and lichen by now, a young man's fancy, Birt's folly. Let the farmers build folds with them.

BRENDAN/BRIGA: So you've not really come back then? What about me?

BIRT: Come. I'll teach you how to fly. You lifted me out of sod and stone. I'll lift you to the stars.

BRENDAN/BRIGA: No you won't.

(*Pause*)

BIRT: Take my hand.

(*Pause. He tells BRENDAN how to play role.*)

You take my hand now.

BRENDAN/BRIGA: I want to be here when he returns.

BIRT: Who?

BRENDAN/BRIGA: Brendan Finnloag.

(*Pause*)

BIRT: But he's not in my dream.

BRENDAN/BRIGA: I've become a novitiate, soon to be a Sister in the Community at Anaghdown. Perhaps, in time... an Abbess.

BIRT: No you haven't!

BRENDAN/BRIGA: He has laid hands upon me.

BIRT: He what . . .? Who?

BRENDAN/BRIGA: Bishop Jarlath at Wethor's Well, where Brendan was baptized.

BIRT: No! That's not how it happened.

(*BIRT grabs shawl from BRENDAN and puts it on, becoming BRIGA.*)

BIRT/BRIGA: Birt, your hands are rough. You've stopped laughing. The wind no longer carries you joy. I am your joy. Too much for any person. Yes, I'll fly with you. Even now I feel my bones becoming hollow. We'll leave now. I'll hold on until. . . you won't let go will you? Brendan is becoming spirit-we'll become feather and wind. Our love will become a whisper to all lovers who lie in sand coves or dance in the glens.

BRENDAN: (*Sharply, cutting him off.*) NO!

BIRT: (*A scream.*) Yes!

(He falls to his knees. Takes off shawl. Wraps his injured hand in it.)

BRENDAN: So stop chasing Leviathans.

BIRT: I've still got one good hand.

BRENDAN: I've come up with a name for him. "Jasconius". He breathes fire and he chases his own tail...

BIRT: The fish?

BRENDAN: But he can never catch it. He's too long, so by the time he nears the tip he's forgotten what he was chasing and stops. There's portent there. You'll remember it, won't you?

BIRT: What?

BRENDAN: The words... Because someday you'll sing a song about this... and other things.

BIRT: I won't. All I'll remember is the empty sea and the smell of ox grease. I will not . . . 'perpetuate' you Brendan Finnloag.

BRENDAN: Already you're beginning to sound like me... words... "perpetuate."

BIRT: All this... (*Waves hand about.*) ...it's become a fool's game.

BRENDAN: Perhaps. Last night I heard voices coming from there...
(*Points West.)*
...echoes that swept over forest and sea.
(*He chants.*)
"On-noee-nangunsett, minnestoba, kaw carrie." Lost souls crying out to the one true God. I heard my name chanted in a thousand tongues: "Come to us, tell us of your Prince of Peace, your. . ." And beyond that the Land of eternal promise. Didn't you hear it, Birt?

BIRT: I wasn't listening.

BRENDAN: Write it down.

BIRT: What?

BRENDAN: What you see. What you hear.

BIRT: Get out!

BRENDAN: I taught you how to read and write.

BIRT: Don't worry. I'll remember all right. Everything. Every tooth I've lost, every blister that drains, every wave that laps against the curragh. (*Holds up hand.*) I'll remember this. Oh, I hear voices too. "You've gone round the bend Birt me Boy. If I was you I'd get off at the nearest isle and catch the next ferry back to misty Eire. You could be lying in a woman's downy arms, Birt, your brain all fuzzy warm from a fine cup of mead, a great sheep dog curled up at your feet. That's paradise, Birt Fenn." It's not something out there, Brendan, it's here and now. Only trouble is I can't remember the last time. . . Or maybe it was the dream I had a while back of sister Briga in the moonlight and the moss. .

BRENDAN: Land Ho!

> (*They both look on in disbelief. BRENDAN falls to his knees. BIRT advances slide projector, the picture is of their ship next to an iceberg.*)

BRENDAN: (*Ecstatic.*) It's the City of God, the new Jerusalem.

BIRT: Aye, it's big enough.

BRENDAN: Shining with the Glory of the Almighty.

BIRT: For three days we sailed toward it.

BRENDAN: Jasper, chalcedony, emerald...

BIRT: It was a mountain of ice.

BRENDAN: Sardonyx, carmelian, chrysolite...

BIRT: Colder than a witch's tit.

BRENDAN: Beryl, topaz, chrysoprase...

BIRT: Your tongue 'd stick to it.

BRENDAN: Jacinth,amethyst, pearls and gold. The light that shines from within... the incorporeal light.

BIRT: It's a reflection, like a piece of cut glass. Feel it. No heat, no fire. The colors-- they'll disappear when the sun sets Look

(*He gets a chisel, hammer and begins "chipping" ice.)*

BRENDAN: Don't do that!

BIRT: Let go! We need fresh water. Taste it.

(*BRENDAN kneels and reverently "tastes" ice. He thinks it's the host.)*

BRENDAN: "...in remembrance of me. . ."

(*BIRT hauls him up.)*

BIRT: Get off your duff-- look, there is land, round there. Would you look!

BRENDAN: "Spiritus Sanctus..."

BIRT: Ice and cairns and ice and rocks and trees withered like dead spiders, and ice. A land of ice.

BRENDAN: (*Slowly.*) Yes. Iceland.

BIRT: (*To audience.*) You watch, they'll remember his words, not mine.

BRENDAN: (*Has a stick and is "measuring".*) Twelve, thirteen, fourteen.

BIRT: If we all pull we'll be on dry land by dusk.

BRENDAN: Nineteen, twenty.

BIRT: What are you doing?

BRENDAN: Measuring its thickness. If it comes to 144 cubits, I'll know.

BIRT: Know what?

BRENDAN: 144 cubits, the thickness of the wall of the Holy City.

(*BIRT takes the stick.*)

BIRT: And this is a cubit? Are you sure it's not this... or this?

BRENDAN: No, I'm not sure.

(*BRENDAN takes stick to measure again. Stops. Sighs.*)

BRENDAN: So close. The City of God, the City of Man. Burned by the cold, burned by the fire. .

(*BIRT grunts. BRENDAN speaks with little resolve.*)

With new resolve we once more headed westward.

(*BIRT brings up slide of Northern Hemisphere. Birt takes a lecture stick in hand, and starts tape recorder. Narrator voice speaks.)*

TAPE/VOICE: The year was 530 or thereabouts. The coast line that of "Irland it Midla" or "Ireland the Great" better known as Iceland. Geologists tell us that historically this was a time of rather violent volcanic activity along the arctic circle here... and here. That's 23 degrees South...

(*BRENDAN stops tape.*)

BRENDAN: Where we encountered a fog as thick.

BIRT: Not yet!

BRENDAN: A fog...

BIRT: Ah no. What about him Brendan? He's my favorite character. I'll set the scene. Volcanoes erupting in the distance, the very "mouth of hell" as you say. Molten rock scattered about-- sizzling. And then you come upon him, a lone figure, burned crisp on one side, blue as ice on the other.

(*He changes the slide to reveal a lone figure on an ice flow-- volcanoes in distance. He puts on a mask that covers half his face--red, hairless. He throws down a large piece of Styrofoam to represent a piece of ice. He puts on a net shirt with thirty pieces of silver attached to it, jangling.)*

BIRT/JUDAS: Brendan, son of Finnloag, purveyor of the Western Isles, Holy man, follower of Jes... (*He stutters*) ...of the high councilor, Blessed Brendan at whose behest the Leviathan shudders, the dead are raised, and before whom the forces of darkness flee... I...

BRENDAN: Silence!

(*Pause. He doesn't look at JUDAS. He says his lines as if they were rote, part of a literary ritual.*)

Who are you?

BIRT/JUDAS: I am unhappy Judas, the most evil trader ever.

BRENDAN: And why are you here.

BIRT/JUDAS: Because I betrayed Jes... my master, for thirty pieces of silver. (*He jangles shirt.*) For this. I was hungry and he left me so. I was thirsty and I remained parched, so now I burn like a lump of molten lead . . .

BRENDAN: But why are you here, right now, floating on ice?

BIRT/JUDAS: His indulgence, His ineffable mercy...

(*BRENDAN turns away.*)

It is the Lord's day-- have you been at sea for so long? I am offered a brief respite in honor of the Lord's resurrection. As long as you tarry I will be allowed to remain here-- at least until sunrise tomorrow.

BRENDAN: (*Turning back.*) So tell me of Him.

BIRT/JUDAS: He looked you in the eye and saw to the black bottom of your soul. He wept once. Never cleaned his plate. Was forgetful about little things. Enjoyed the rain. Sorrowed after small creatures. Was careful where he placed his hands. Slept little but deeply. He took large steps so you had to hurry at times to keep up. Didn't manage money well. Would sometimes stop in the middle of sentences as if he was listening to . . . somewhere else. He had a Northern accent, clipped his vowels-- never heard anyone ask him to repeat himself however. He demanded his private time. Had great social but little political awareness and his agenda was... ambiguous. That's what I knew then.

BRENDAN: And now?

BIRT/JUDAS: Now I hear and listen only to myself. What did you say your name was?

BRENDAN: Brendan.

BIRT/JUDAS: Ah, yes. And I suppose there will be many other travelers like yourself following in your footsteps. I followed in His and look where it got me. My mother said I should have been a farmer. Misery loves company but I tire of the cries of Annas, Pilate, Herod. . . others. .

BRENDAN: I don't plan on staying.

(*He starts to paddle off.*)

BIRT/JUDAS: Until sunrise. You won't be leaving before that will you?
(*Shows silver coins.*)
Are you interested in learning about these?

BRENDAN: Tell me.

BIRT/JUDAS: Each represents a good deed. Here is one which tells of a cloth I gave to a leper when I was procurator for the Lord. It wasn't mine to take, however, belonged to Nathaniel. And here-- arranged to have those Gadarene farmers reimbursed after their pigs dashed off the cliff at Jes... his command. Of the twelve, I'm the only one that's been invited back. Here, one for never having taken the Lord's name in vain. Here's one for trying to give them back. I did you know, I tried . . . but it's never been . . . recognized. It's surprising how much of your life just doesn't. . .seem to count. Here, one for having kissed my Master. The world has misinterpreted this one. . . has nothing to do with betrayal. . . but rather with . . . I was saying goodbye . . . a gesture immortalized but totally misconstrued. Feel how heavy this one is, even now it burns a hole through my breast, through the ice. .
(*He yells.)*
Brendan, take them, take them back, sell them as indulgences along with splinters from the cross and hairs from His beard. Throw them in the sea. Cap teeth with them. Lay them on the eyes of the dead.

BRENDAN: Cast them away yourself.

BIRT/JUDAS: I can't. They weigh too much.

BRENDAN: I am not an instrument of forgiveness.

BIRT/JUDAS: But he cherishes you. Surely you can take on a part of my burden, surely you are called to that. We're all in this together, you know.

BRENDAN: Only Christ carries the yoke of our sins.

BIRT/JUDAS: I know all that. I don't need any homilies, I have a much better idea of His eternal plan than you have. All I'm asking...

(*BRENDAN turns away.*)

Curse you Brendan Finnloag. Curse the day you were conceived and the sinful womb that conceived you. Curse your journey. May you preach only to crabs and snails. May your boat be rent asunder by the dark terror of the sea and may you be eaten and spit out and eaten again until all memory or notion or word or gesture of your being is forgotten and all that remains of you is nothingness. Let it be!

(*Silence.*)

Say something!

(*Silence.*)

Brendan!

(*Silence. JUDAS holds his ears from the silence.*)

Look, I'm sorry. I take it back, all the words... it's just, well, you've caught me at a bad time. Uh, surely there is something else you'd like to know. I was with him for the better part of two years. I...

BRENDAN; How can an incorporeal light burn corporeally in a corporeal creature?

BIRT/JUDAS; What's that? Metaphysics? I'm a pragmatist Brendan, I keep count of things. Ask me what he laughed at or what he said as he cried out in his sleep.

BRENDAN: How did he cope with it?

BIRT/JUDAS; The incorporeal fire? Well, I don't imagine that he... I mean he never said anything directly...

BRENDAN: Why was he not consumed? Why aren't we?

BIRT/JUDAS: By God's Holy fire? I wasn't around at Pentecost, I missed all of that, still a mystery to me.

(*BRENDAN turns away.*)

But I can take a guess. Being sinless, as they say, the fire within burned pure, nothing to burn up, no baggage, no refuse, nothing handed down, nothing hidden, pure goodness-non quenchable.

BRENDAN: Yes, but what about us?

BIRT/JUDAS: I burn everyday Brendan, scorched on an hourly basis, forks and pincers, my flesh is ripped and torn... ad infinitum...

BRENDAN: But within...

BIRT/JUDAS: Within? Within there is nothing. Ex nihilio.

BRENDAN: For you?

BIRT/JUDAS: For all of us.

BRENDAN: Unhappy Judas.

BIRT/JUDAS: Wandering Brendan. (*Pause.*) Take me with you. On windless days I'll blow into your sail. In tempests I'll act as ballast. I've studied the stars. Haven't you heard?-- I bring good luck to waifs and wanderers. I'll entertain you so with stories of lost souls and the vagaries of man's misdeeds that you'll dare not sleep for fear of what you might miss. Take my hand, Brendan.

BRENDAN: Hoist sail I Come about!

BIRT/JUDAS: Brendan! Now I will be with you always, a black mark be upon your forehead, the mark of an unrequited soul denied. Take my hand! Brendan'

> (*He screams, Re-verb. BIRT noisily gets out of costume. He gets a piece of bread and messily smears grease on it. He sits next to BRENDAN.*)

BIRT: You want a bite?
> (*BRENDAN shakes his head.*)

Last o' the lard.
> (*Dips his fingers in, sucks.*)

Not bad. Softens the crust.
> (*Knocks bread.*)

Like a brick.
> (*Loud eating noises.*)

Wouldn't of taken much-- just to stretch out your hand like this. "Grab on Judas, we're on our way to hell anyway so your company is welcome". I would of done it. There's always room for another poor blighter. Help with the chores." God knows no one else around here does. (*Pause.*) Wouldn't have taken that much, Brendan. Sure you wouldn't want a bite?

(*BRENDAN stands. New slide of the Sargossa Sea, eels, vines climbing up the side of the ship.)*

BRENDAN: Later we passed through the sea of weeds. We ate eels and skimmed fresh water off the top. Birt danced.

(BIRT dances over the side of the ship.)

BIRT: Lookee, Bren. I'm walking, no I'm dancing on water. You think that's how your savior did it? Found a patch of weeds wove so thick?

(*He dances and sings.)*

COME MY LASS,
WHY SIT YE THERE SO STILL?
COME RUN WITH ME,
THROUGH FOREST GREEN,
AND DANCE WE TWO UPON THIS HILL.

COME MY LASS,
WHY SIT YE THERE SO STILL?
COME RUN WITH ME,
OR YOU'LL BE CAUGHT
BY DEATHS DARK CHILL.

(*Pause. He stops dancing.)*

Why won't you dance with me Brendan? Do you good. It's a way of laughing without laughing, of crying without shedding a tear. Maybe you won't 'cause it's somethin' I got that you don't. Take my hand, Brendan, I'm willing to share it with you.

(*BRENDAN considers the invitation rejects the idea and turns towards audience.*)

BRENDAN: Later still we sailed into a bank of fog so thick it was like breathing in the sea itself.

(*Slide of ship sailing into fog. BIRT shivers.*)

BIRT: It reminds me of home.

BRENDAN: Tralee.

BIRT: Ay, there at the bottom o' the hill. You'd wake covered with dew and mold.

BRENDAN: Here, take my robe.

BIRT: No. I like being reminded, it gives me an edge.

BRENDAN: It's there you know, just the other side of the fog.

BIRT: What?

BRENDAN: The Land of Promise.

BIRT: Paradise you mean?

BRENDAN: Ay!

BIRT: Say's you.

BRENDAN: The land of everlasting where man exists in the eternal present.

BIRT: Sounds boring to me-- sittin' around pickin' fruit, waitin' for nothin'.

BRENDAN: Where the lion shall lie down with the lamb and where the viper shall become the play thing of children.

BIRT: I like a bit of struggle, I do. Just a bit. Somethin' to overcome. You haul rocks out of the field, but then you bring the barley in, barley which had been growed with water, sun and the sweat of your brow. You hear a woman screaming with the birth of a wee bairn, but when it's over you carry new life in your arms and you're ready to do it all over again. I tell you it might be a curse but it's also a blessing. What good's the joy of something if you don't have the pain to show you what it's worth? I could take two, maybe three weeks of lying around doing nothing and I'd be ready to see the salt spray coming up over the prow. Movement. A bit of shoulders on with whatever. It's this cold I can't stand, grey, like the belly of a worm. (*Pause.*)

So what say, ye, Brendan son of Finnloag?

BRENDAN: To what?

BIRT: To all I've just said. You've always got to have the last word in.

BRENDAN: I too hate the grayness.

BIRT: That's it?

BRENDAN: You conjure images in the mist. Your fears. You dwell within. The emptiness...

BIRT: Aye, it's then you need a wife.

BRENDAN: Or a friend.

(*He takes robe and puts it over Birt's shoulders, who does not respond, but neither does he throw it off. The lights get suddenly brighter.*)

Look! It's there! The Land of Promise. Bring her about, Birt!

BIRT: Like any other barren shore. Scrub. A few crabs.

BRENDAN: A land of perpetual light.

BIRT: Same sun. Same moon. Same tide. Same...

BRENDAN: *(Grabs BIRT.)* You'll tell them what I see. .

(*BIRT frees himself. Pushes button on tape recorder. The following sequence is synchronized with the tape player. The TAPE/VOICE has that professional travelogue sound to* it . *Irish music in the background.*)

TAPE/VOICE: "For periods varying between two and seven years Brendan is said to have explored the western ocean. Some accounts place his landing in Newfoundland and others mention the Virginian Capes."

BRENDAN: On disembarking from the boat we saw a wide land full of trees bearing fruit as in autumn time. For forty days we reconnoitered the whole land and could not find the end of it.

BIRT: Flies as big as your thumb. Animals abounded, that be true, but as dumb as the animals of Eire-- no lions or lambs to be seen.

TAPE/VOICE: "There is said to be proof in indigenous remains that

Irishmen had settled in America centuries before the Vikings landed or the Spanish sighted its shore."

BRENDAN: We came to a broad river flowing through the middle of the land. I said to my brethren: "We cannot cross this river and we do not know the size of this land." It was then when a youth of the land came and embraced us and with great joy called each by his name saying:" Happy are they that live in your house. They shall praise you from generation to generation. There before you lies the land which you have sought for a long time. You could not find it immediately because God wanted to show you his varied secrets in the great ocean."

BIRT: We met the inhabitants. Dark skinned men who dressed in rags and wore necklaces of bone. Brendan preached of Jesu, the savior of mankind. They squatted like this and drew pictures in the sand.

TAPE/VOICE: "When Cortez and his six hundred landed in 1519 they were amazed to find their arrival hailed as the fulfillment of a native tradition. They were told that, many centuries before, one whom the natives called Quetzalcoatl-- the Precious-- had come from some "holy isle" of the northeast, in a boat with "wings" or sails. According to their tradition he was a tall white man, advanced in years, with broad forehead, black hair and beard, and he wore a long garment, over which hung a mantle marked with crosses. For several years he remained in their country teaching the divine faith."

BRENDAN: I was told to return to the land of my birth bringing with me some of the fruit and precious stones that hung on the trees and lay in the ground. This man, who I suspected of being an angel, said to me: "The final day of your pilgrimage draws near so that you may sleep with your fathers. After the passage of many times this land will become known to your successors, when persecution of the Christians shall have come."

BIRT: I heard no voices. I stayed on the beach near the curragh and let Brendan wander ashore. I sewed and greased the hides. (*Loudly.*) Brendan! If you don't come now winter will set and we'll ne'er make it back. I be leaving without you, Holy Man.

(*He spits.*)

TAPE/VOICE: In many ancient maps St. Brendan's Island, under various denominations, was marked in the western sea and to some extent influenced Columbus.

BRENDAN: You see?

BIRT: You can swim if you like. I'm leaving.

BRENDAN: I returned home directly.

BIRT: I won't spend time telling you about the return journey. It were iust more of the same.

TAPE/VOICE: (*The characters run in place.*) Brendan's return home was the signal for great rejoicings. Crowds flocked to welcome the Christian Ulysses whose reappearance had the air of a return from the dead. It was the year 552 and he rushed to the nunnery at Anaghdown to see his sister Briga.

(*BRENDAN and BIRT rush forward and yell in unison--reverb effect.*)

BRENDAN and BIRT: Briga!

(*They look out. BRENDAN grabs a cloak, which identifies him as BRIGA, and approaches BIRT.*)

BRENDAN/BRIGA: You've come back. Stand up straight. Now turn around. Yes. Strong arms. And your eyes... are they bluer?

BIRT: The sea does that.

BRENDAN/BRIGA: But your back... bent...

BIRT: The sea does that also.

BRENDAN/BRIGA: I've been to the cottage. It's overgrown. The moss... Two goats live there now.

BIRT: Good. They've kept it warm. With their dung we'll make a garden. I'll cut down the trees, let the sunshine in. We'll dance in the meadow.

BRENDAN/BRIGA: Then you don't know. But of course, how could you? I've married.

BIRT: (*Pause. Not hearing.*) Seven coppers a day. I can buy a servant who will cook.

BRENDAN/BRIGA: Jesus is my husband. He is the only one that I dance with now. We are a small order-- we serve only those who serve the sea. Come work with us Birt.

(*BIRT screams "No!" and violently wrenches the shawl from BRENDAN.*)

BIRT: You knew this would happen. You knew that if I left she'd run to the strong arms of your shepherd. All right! But tell it like it was, Brendan. Stinking of salt muck you ran to the gates of the nunnery at Anaghdown and yelled with what voice you had left.

(*Like before BRENDAN runs in slow motion, and his following yell is re-verbed.*)

BRENDAN: Briga!

(*BIRT has thrown cloak over his head and shoulders, has grabbed a gnarled staff, and slowly hobbles toward BRENDAN.*)

BIRT/BRIGA: Shut-it! Ye'll wake the sisters. Away with you!
(*Pause. She looks closer. Walks slowly toward him.*)
Brendan? Oh Brendan... so you've come home.
(*He rushes towards her.*)
No. Keep your distance. You've done well enough for these last... seven... nine... years. I stopped counting long ago. If you want to make a contribution put it there in the bowl, otherwise you'd better be off...

(*She wipes her nose with her sleeve, you can't tell whether she is crying or just sniffling, she turns to go.*)

BRENDAN: Briga! What has happened?
BIRT/BRIGHA: (*She has gone mad.*) I should of known when the crickets left the house. "Ashen tree, ashen tree." He took my little ones. Angelica and broom, coltsfoot and poppy, I tried them all, cures and curses. Their little breaths became a whisper, then naught. If you'd been here with the touch of God there on your thumb, things woulda been different.
(*She exits, chanting.*)
"There came three ladies out of the East,
One with fire and two with frost.
Out with the fire, in with the frost."

(Sound of wind howling in distance. BRENDAN sinks to his knees. BIRT has discarded shawl and is standing over him sprinkling snow flakes on his head and shoulders.)

BRENDAN: It's cold, Birt.

(BIRT throws cloak over his shoulders.)

BIRT: Here, wear my robe.

BRENDAN: You've taken all that I have, taken it all away.

BIRT: No more than you've taken from me.

(BRENDAN crawls and hits slide projector. Blank screen.)

You see? It's all over.

BIRT: There is still more to come.

BRENDAN: It's all been for naught-- the journey. Naught for me, naught for her, naught for Christ.

BIRT: Would you listen to him. He sails to the new world, starts a hundred cells, monasteries, missionary schools, seminaries. . . and says it's all for naught. Just like him.

BRENDAN: Cold. Teach me how to dance.

BIRT: I thought you'd never ask. Best thing for a chill. Stand.

(BRENDAN stands.)

Now clear your mind of all things old and all things dead. Feel the earth and the wind. Lift your knee, like this, lift up, a hop and down-- now the other. That's it. Again. Take my hand.

(They dance as BIRT coaches him. Irish music has started in background, nothing too joyful, a bit mournful, a lament, but fast enough to move to.)

BIRT: And dance. Dance for Birt who is lost, for Briga who is empty, for Brendan who is alone.

(*BRENDAN dances slowly by himself, not a pretty dance, but ultimately it is a dance not to himself but to his Lord.*)

BRENDAN: For God who is breath, for He who is froth and wave and depth and height...

BIRT: No! Dance for Brendan.

BRENDAN: Lord of motion, a new song that never ends. Dance for creation-- for mountain, and field, leaf, tree, mouse and snail, for...

(*He dances, more ecstatic, shouting words, stepping higher. BIRT finally grabs him, but even as he hold him BRENDAN continues to jerk and move in dance movements.*)

BIRT: Stop! Hold damn you! Dance, for Birt, he who is your brother...

BRENDAN: Yes. Birt. My brother.

(*He holds out his arms to embrace BIRT.*)

BIRT: (*Angry and upset.*) Not your brother in spirit, but your brother in flesh.

BRENDAN: What?

BIRT: Ay, you'll listen now. It was the year of our Lord, 483 when Finnloag came down the hill and took my mother in the wet leaves, laid her down in the muck of the earth and mixed breath and seed and sweat and made me. Brother. Conceived me the same night he made you up there, atop the hill. It t'were all seen by Fenn. It was

BIRT: Fenn who looked in your window and spied on Cara, Cara of the bright breasts and who was caught. Yes. it was Fenn who was caught and dragged down the hill by Finnloag and made to watch as he took my mother in the peat while Fenn cried. But who is to say that the lightening and the shining that came nine months later weren't for me? Who is to say?

BRENDAN: You?

BIRT: Your brother.

BRENDAN: And Briga?

BIRT: I know-- my half sister. The gods would frown upon that. But blood aside I would of had her. I loved her, Brendan, god how I loved her. Wherever she touched me I burned. I still burn. You've got YOUR fire-- I've got mine.

(BRENDAN turns away, bent over as if he might wretch. Slowly he turns, straightens up holds his hand out to BIRT. He speaks hoarsely.)

BRENDAN: Brother. . .

BIRT: Oh no. It's too late, there's too much blood, too much sweat, too much water passed between us. I've learned to hate your snores at night, the hissing of your prayers. I know you too well, Brendan, too much like a brother, so keep away.

(BRENDAN senses the tremendous anger and hurt in BIRT and roughly embraces him, holding on for dear life. BIRT struggles to get free. Suddenly BRENDAN stiffens, staggers away holding his chest, breathing with large gulps of raspy breath. He falls. BIRT watches him.)

BIRT: It's over Brendan. Get up now.

(Pause.)

That was a nice touch. It's time to take your bow and pack it in.

(Pause.)

Brendan.

(He moves quickly to him. Kneels beside him and takes him in his arms.)

Come on, Brendan, enough of this. It's not fair. I tell you of Mum and Finnloag and all, I tell you that, and now you . . it's something we have to work out. . .dwell on... it doesn't just end here.

(Shaking him.)

I tell you it's not fair.

BRENDAN: So cold...

BIRT: Here now, I'll keep you warm.

BRENDAN: The fire... how can an incorporeal light burn corporeally...? So cold, Birt.

BIRT: I'm here. Brendan, listen to me. You can't go now. I need you to hate. I can't stand the aloneness.

BRENDAN: "Commend to God in your prayers my departure from this life."

BIRT: Brendan, I don't pray.

BRENDAN: "I fear as I pass away all alone, and as the journey is darksome, I fear the unknown region, the presence of the King, the sentence of the Judge." The light? Where. . .?

BIRT: It's there-- hold on. A days sail, that's all.

BRENDAN: Darksome...

BIRT: Just over the horizon. Don't let go.

> (*BRENDAN stretches his hand out as if seeing it. He is lit in a special light, a special iridescence.*)

BRENDAN: (*He caresses BIRT's face.*) Sing my song.

BIRT: (*A scream of denial.*) No!

> (*BRENDAN dies. BIRT weeps over the body he is holding. He carries it to the sail and shrouds BRENDAN in it. He says the following speech as a eulogy.*)

You pray for me, Brendan, friend, as you stand before the throne of Your God. Pray for my doubt. Pray for my emptiness. My darkness and anger come from the loins of your father. I have lived fitfully in the yawn of your shadow. But what light I have seen, what thoughts I have thought, these I attribute to you, my sailorman.

> (*Music up. BIRT weeps. He sings/recites the following fulfilling his destiny as the chronicler of Brendan's Journey.*)

BIRT:
HE WAS BORN ATOP A HILL,
IN THE GREEN GREEN OF TRALEE.
HE GREW A STRONG STOUT LAD,
WHO YEARNED TO GO TO SEA.

(*Chorus.*)
SAIL BRENDAN, SAIL,
SAIL THROUGH WIND AND WAVE,
SAIL FAR MY FRIEND, SAIL,
BE BRAVE MY FRIEND BE BRAVE.

HE SAILED INTO SEAS UNKNOWN,
TO THE BLUE, BLUE OCEANS RIM.
HE SHOUTED "LAND A HOY"
AND SANG TO THE WIND HIS HYMN.

HIS TEARS THEY FELL TO THE WAKE,
HIS HEART IT BURNED FOR THE LOST,
"COME ABOUT MY FELLOW MAN, COME ABOUT,
ALL OF YE WHO ARE SIN TOSSED".

(*Chorus. Lights dim. Music under.*)

THE END

Made in the
USA
Lexington, KY

55596233R00033